IMAGES
of America

MANSFIELD TOWNSHIP, BURLINGTON COUNTY

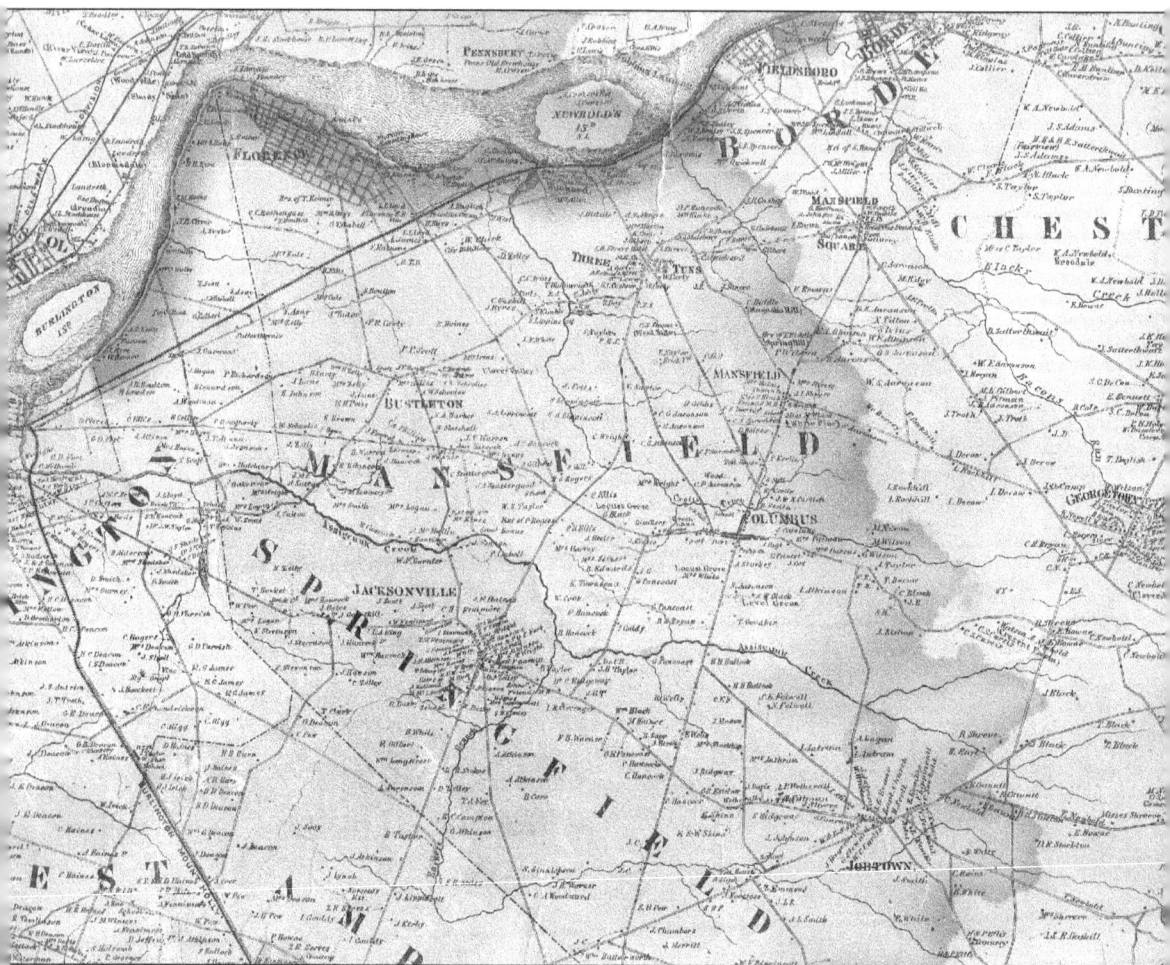

This is an 1865 school wall map of Mansfield Township. (Courtesy of David Potts.)

On the cover: In this 1943 photograph of the Columbus Field Day parade where it ends at the Columbus Civic and Athletic Association, members of the Mansfield Township 4-H Club pose on their float. Posing from left to right are Roger Armstrong, Bill Aaronson, Delores Priedel, Harold Potts, Calvin Stevenson, Franklin Wainwright, George "Bud" Aaronson, and Maurice Stevenson. (Courtesy of Franklin Wainwright.)

IMAGES
of America

MANSFIELD TOWNSHIP, BURLINGTON COUNTY

Mansfield Township Historical Society Book Committee

ARCADIA
PUBLISHING

Published by Arcadia Publishing
Charleston SC, Chicago IL, Portsmouth NH, San Francisco CA

Library of Congress Catalog Card Number: 2008936590

For all general information contact Arcadia Publishing at:
Telephone 843-853-2070
Fax 843-853-0044
E-mail sales@arcadiapublishing.com
For customer service and orders:
Toll-Free 1-888-313-2665

Visit us on the Internet at www.arcadiapublishing.com

The Keeler Oak, a majestic white oak, stands proudly at 88 feet with a drip line of 120 feet. This 300-year-old tree located on Petticoat Bridge Road was witness to the Colonial troops and Hessian soldiers as they marched through Black Horse (Columbus) down Petticoat Bridge Road where the famous skirmish took place during the Revolutionary War. The Keeler Oak, affectionately named after the owners of the farm where it stands, serves as Mansfield's logo. (Courtesy of Claudia Teal.)

CONTENTS

ACKNOWLEDGMENTS

A work of this nature was made possible through the cooperative efforts of the Mansfield Township Historical Society, the Columbus Grange No. 58, and the wonderful, caring individuals who live in the area of Mansfield Township. The collection of articles and photographs so meticulously preserved by these two organizations and individuals throughout the years made this publication possible. The effort and dedication of Janet Aaronson, Pearl Tusim, and Roy Parcels in canvassing the community soliciting additional images from the archives of area residents is appreciated. Born and raised in Mansfield Township, Alice Elliott was helpful in identifying individuals and actions in many of the images. Thanks to Marge Ford who interviewed individuals and recorded the history associated with their photographs. Expressions of gratitude are extended to Janet Aaronson, Alice Elliott, and Marion Tallon, who wrote the text for this volume and the script that accompanies each photograph. The efforts of Abigail Hemmes toward the completion of the volume are appreciated. Many thanks are extended to Dave Potts and Bob Tallon. Their knowledge of technology along with their pleasing demeanor made this adventure into publishing a rewarding learning experience. The leadership of Claudia Teal organized, coordinated, and guided us through the entire process from beginning to end. Her unassuming, positive outlook gave us assurance of a pleasing finished product.

INTRODUCTION

Established as a constabulary in 1688 and incorporated in 1798, the history of Mansfield Township originates with the arrival from England of three vessels three miles to the west at Burlington on the Delaware River in 1677 and 1678: the *Kent*, the *Shield*, and the flie-boat *Martha*. Passengers aboard these vessels were wealthy English landowners and members of the Society of Friends (Quakers). A number of these peaceful, sturdy, courageous travelers settled in the area of Mansfield Township. Here they formed small settlements throughout the township, lived peacefully and cooperatively among the population of Native Americans, and cleared land for roads, dwellings, and farming. The courage and sturdiness of these early arrivals is characterized by one of Mansfield's settlers. Thomas Scattergood arrived from England with his wife and a deed for 500 acres of land along Craft's Creek. With no habitable structure on his acreage, he and his wife took up residence in a cavelike earthen dwelling until they were able to build a house. In the spirit of their parents, the children of these sturdy, courageous individuals built schools and churches, established businesses, served politically in New Jersey's and the nation's legislative bodies, and fought for freedom. Among the passengers aboard the three vessels were William Black, Thomas Wright, Samuel Taylor, Godfrey Hancock and family, Thomas Potts, Godfrey and John Newbold, Thomas Kirby, and William Biddle. Some descendants of these early settlers reside in Mansfield Township today.

In December 1776, the American Revolution seemed on the verge of collapse until a skirmish that never reached historic proportions took place at a small bridge in Mansfield Township. On December 23, on orders from Gen. George Washington to pull Hessian troops encamped in nearby Bordentown south and away from the proximity of Trenton, colonists attacked a small outpost situated on Petticoat Bridge Road. The skirmish lasted two days. This act was successful in luring the Hessians southward as they pursued the American colonists into Mount Holly. This skirmish assured Washington's success in the battle of Trenton, as the Hessians were too far removed from Trenton to come to the aid of British troops stationed there.

In the mid-1700s, Mansfield Township consisted of one town and five villages. Located geographically in the center of the township is the town of Columbus. Columbus has had three names throughout the years, the first being Encroaching Corners. An 1875 map reveals a misalignment of streets that comprised the town's main intersection. Consequently, it caused difficulty moving cattle and livestock through this intersection on their way to grazing and market. Thus the town was named Encroaching Corners. The second name was Black Horse. This name came into use as the stagecoach stop, located in the center of town, was at the Black Horse Tavern. In 1827, the town council officially changed the name to Columbus.

Prior to 1834, the current village of Georgetown was called Foolstown. In 1834, the village was named Georgetown in honor of New Jersey congressman George Sykes, who lived a few miles to the east on Mount Pleasant Road between Georgetown and Columbus. Georgetown boasted of the first department store in New Jersey that contained an elevator. Owned by the Frazer brothers, the store handled all kinds of merchandise. The brothers bought everything local farmers produced and sold everything the farmers needed. A. J. Keeley's Hotel in Georgetown was the stop for the daily stagecoach run between Columbus and Burlington. Georgetown was a complete community with a post office, a hotel, a lodge hall, a large carriage manufacturing business, a church, and a school.

Just north of Columbus on Route 206 is the village of Mansfield Square. A Quaker meetinghouse, built in 1812, along with a school and a scattering of houses made this an active settlement.

The village of Rising Sun Square is located just a few miles north of Mansfield Square. It is situated at Mansfield's northern boundary. Originally it was a stop on the stagecoach run along the historic Old York Road. A hotel with a sign depicting a rising sun gave the village its name. A school and a few houses were scattered throughout the village. Hessian troops were billeted in the Rising Sun Hotel during the American Revolution.

Traveling west on Old York Road for several miles, one arrives at the village of Hedding, originally known as Three Tuns. The stagecoach route that transported passengers between Perth Amboy and Burlington made stops for rest and refreshment at the Three Tuns Tavern, which was located at the crossroads in the village. Consequently, the area was identified as Three Tuns. In addition to the tavern, Three Tuns had a church, a school, a blacksmith shop, a store, a cluster of homes, and a wheelwright business. This settlement was later renamed Hedding in honor of the Methodist bishop who served the church there.

The village of Kinkora, located along the Delaware River, was the terminus of the Camden and Amboy Railroad, and the Kinkora Springfield Railroad was added in the late 1800s. With the railroads established in the area in addition to large shops for the repair of locomotives and the building of railroad cars and other commercial enterprises, Kinkora became a busy, thriving commercial area.

The introduction of the railroad in Mansfield Township during the mid-1800s ushered in an era of affluence. Farmers were now able to transport their produce to more distant markets. Transportation became available for individuals who were employed out of town. Schooling in Mansfield extended only through grade eight. Railroad travel gave students the opportunity to complete their high school educations in nearby towns where high schools were available.

During the first half of the 1900s, Mansfield residents turned to America's favorite pastime, baseball. Stress associated with World War I and the Great Depression was relieved during the excitement of viewing a competitive baseball game between the Mansfield home team and neighboring teams. Driven by their enthusiasm for the sport, Mansfield citizens formed the Columbus Civic and Athletic Association (CC&AA). The objective of the CC&AA was to raise funds to field a baseball team and to build a community clubhouse and a pool. These sports enthusiasts were successful in meeting their objectives. In 1939, the CC&AA was instrumental in the founding of Field Day. Field Day has become a 70-year tradition in the township. Each year on the second Saturday in June, Field Day commences with a parade and culminates with a baseball game and numerous games and races.

During the years of World War II from 1941 to 1945, Mansfield's young men and several young women were in uniform. On the home front, families planted victory gardens, juggled rationing stamps, and purchased victory bonds. With a railroad terminus in Columbus, Mansfield citizens met trains journeying to Camp Dix and delivered cookies and other goodies to military enlistees and soldiers traveling to the military base.

Today Mansfield Township retains its small-town rural atmosphere while providing all of the amenities offered in larger, more populated cities.

One

PEOPLE AND PLACES

Ye Auld Columbus Inn,
Columbus, N. J.

Built in 1812, the Columbus Inn is located on the corner of West Main Street and New York Avenue. It replaced the first Black Horse (Columbus) Tavern built in 1761. This tavern was an important stop on the run that extended from Cooper's Ferry to New York City. A bell located on the front porch rang to announce an approaching stagecoach. There was once an A&P store in the west end of the building. Former owners, John Aaronson, E. A. Atkinson, and J. Kerlin actually believed that ghosts roamed the establishment. (Courtesy of Mansfield Township Historical Society.)

treet Scene looking North, Columbus, N. J.

This picture, taken at the corner and looking north along New York Avenue, shows a log pillar of the Columbus Inn, and next to the pillar is a pole with a bell at the top. The bell alerted travelers that the stagecoach had arrived. Earlier maps also refer to New York Avenue as Union Street and Bordentown Street. (Courtesy of Mansfield Township Historical Society.)

Street Scene, Columbus, N. J.

This picture was taken at the entrance to Mill Lane and looks west along Main Street. The house shown at the far right was once the parsonage for the Baptist church. It was later the home of Ryland Croshaw. Elmer Lippincott now owns the second house. (Courtesy of Tom Sahol.)

Street Scene looking East,
Columbus, N. J.

This is a view of East Main Street in the late 1800s. The first house on the left is still standing next to the Corner House Tavern. The house on the right with the three steps is also standing but with a new porch and steps on the side. (Courtesy of Mansfield Township Historical Society.)

Street Scene,
Columbus, N. J.

This is a view of West Main Street taken at the intersection. The building on the left was a store, and on the right are several small stores. All were torn down for a bank building on the left and a driveway on the right for the Columbus Inn. (Courtesy of Tom Sahol.)

This house, located at 10 New York Avenue, sits on a half-acre lot. Mrs. Scott and her daughter Anna owned it. Anna later married David Allen Meirs Sr., and they had a son named David. (Courtesy of Mansfield Township Historical Society.)

Located on West Main Street, this was the house of Thomas Larzelere from 1810 to 1867. Larzelere was an architect who helped draw the plans for the Capitol building in Washington, D.C. (Courtesy of John LeRoy Parcels Sr.)

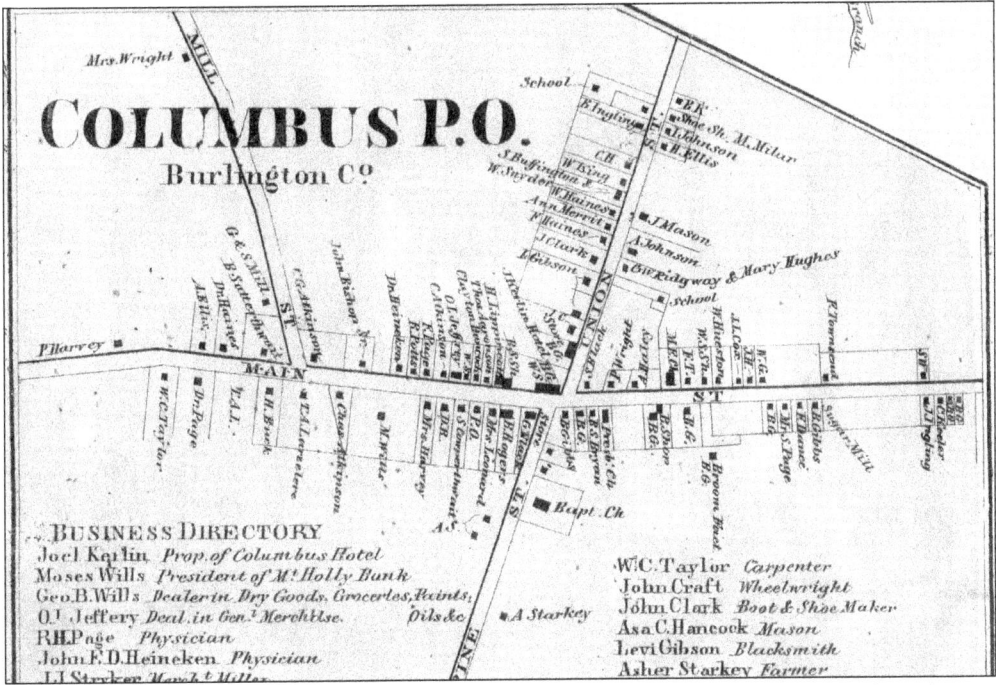

This is a map of Columbus made in 1895 that shows a directory of businesses and residences. Notice Pine Street at the south end of Columbus is now named Atlantic Avenue. (Courtesy of Stone and Pomeroy of Philadelphia.)

Archer's Store, seen here around 1920, is located on East Main Street in Columbus. The first telephone in Columbus was installed here. (Courtesy of Mansfield Township Historical Society.)

13

Sharp's Agricultural Woodwork and Machine Shop, located on New York Avenue behind Dobbin's Drug Store, is shown here around 1895. (Courtesy of Mansfield Township Historical Society.)

Shown here is a corn stub cutter exhibited at the Mount Holly Fair Grounds in 1900. It was manufactured at Sharp's machine shop, where Jack Sharp, blacksmith, was an innovator of agricultural implements. (Courtesy of Mansfield Township Historical Society.)

The Bishop and Page lumber dealers shipped its products from the railroad depot loading area pictured here. The railroad depot was located in Columbus from the mid-1800s to the mid-1900s. (Courtesy of Jackie Fama.)

Pictured is equipment painted by William Craft, who specialized in gold leaf lettering in his business as a carriage painter, located on New York Avenue. (Courtesy of Rosemary Craft.)

The American Store, located on the corner of West Main Street and Atlantic Avenue, sold groceries until the 1950s when Mr. Smith was the grocer. This corner was a social gathering spot for Columbus residents. (Courtesy of Pat Wright.)

Columbus Water Company workmen are digging the well where the water tower would stand for many years. The cone-shaped building on the left is called a cistern. Water was distributed from this building on the way to houses in Columbus. This was an early form of water purification. The water company was owned by the Carslake family then sold to the American Water Company. (Courtesy of Robert Carslake.)

Postmaster Chas. Carslake Residence, Columbus, N. J.

The property of Edward L. Carslake and his wife, Emily, came to the family by a land grant. This farm was used for dairying and produced feed for the animals. The barn was unique in that it was a cellar barn. It was sold to the William Shinn family who continue to farm. (Courtesy of Mansfield Township Historical Society.)

Charles S. Carslake (1873–1933) was a lifelong resident of Columbus. He was a justice of the peace and a prohibition agent. During the 1930s, attempts to bribe him were made. On one raid, more than 1,000 cases of liquor were confiscated. The offender never came to trial because the liquor disappeared. Charles was found dead in the Jersey Pine Barrens. The circumstances surrounding his death remain a mystery. (Courtesy of Janet Aaronson.)

William Carslake stands next to his grandmother Mary Carslake who is holding her granddaughter Sarah. Seated is Edward L. Carslake. William is holding a metal mechanical toy received as a Christmas gift. (Courtesy of Janet Aaronson.)

William Carslake, the local game warden, lived on East Main Street with his wife, Helen, and five children, William, Robert, Joseph, Irving, and Ruth. He passed away at the very young age of 45. (Courtesy of Bill Montrey.)

Brothers William (left) and Edward L. Carslake pose in 1937 after a day of hunting. The brothers are shown outside the house of their mother, Mary, on West Main Street in Columbus. (Courtesy of Bill Montrey.)

The young Irving Carslake is pictured with his father, William. (Courtesy of Bill Montrey.)

This is grandfather Edwin Wilson holding the horse for sisters Frances and Leila Wilson. Frances married Oliver Burtis, and Leila married Frank P. Smith. Both sisters and their families lived on New York Avenue. (Courtesy of Jackie Fama.)

Frances and Oliver Burtis's daughter Leona is shown at age one in her high-buttoned shoes. (Courtesy of Jackie Fama.)

Frank P. Smith owned a meat market on East Main Street next to A. N. Dobbins Drug Store. His daughter Alberta owned the Smith's Bus Company. (Courtesy of Jackie Fama.)

Having a fine time in a small place. Clara.

A. N. Dobbins Drug Store was located on East Main Street and New York Avenue. It closed in 1905. The building is now the Corner House Tavern. (Courtesy of David Potts.)

21

The Smith's Bus Company provided public transportation along with transportation to and from school for Mansfield's students. (Courtesy of Jackie Fama.)

In 1945, one of the Smith's buses unloads at the elementary school on Locust Avenue. The building in the background was the first school built in Columbus. The children from left to right are Mary Kira, Wally Reed, Lois Reed, Ted Bishop, Grace Parker, Ed Parker, John Kira, Sarah Wright, Ken Parker, John Vancza, driver Woody Rossell, Barbara Vancza, unidentified, Allen Reed, Pat Wright, Ralph Parker, and Addison Reed. (Courtesy of Jackie Fama.)

The Burtis family gathers for a snapshot in 1958. Charles and Elizabeth Burtis raised five girls. He was a butcher and owned a store on West Main Street. (Courtesy of Jackie Fama.)

Residence of Geo. Black, Columbus, N. J.

The history of this 12-room Victorian house, located on West Main Street, is traced to 1900 when Harvey Thomas purchased it. In 1911, Elizabeth Black purchased it, and it remained in the Black family until 1945. The Blacks were prominent farmers in Mansfield. William Black served as township committeeman from 1787 to 1820. He had eight children. Black's Creek and the Columbus Steam Mill Company were associated with his family. In 1945, Myrtle and Howard Flurer purchased the house and raised son Jack and daughter Dorothy here. Howard Flurer was a carpenter and had a sawmill on this property. (Courtesy of Alice Elliott.)

Born in 1881, William M. Craft was involved in the Burlington County Democratic Party. He started the Craft Builders business. Crafts Creek, which traverses Mansfield Township, was named after his family. (Courtesy of Rosemary Craft.)

Zilpah B. Craft, descendant of the Tantum family in Georgetown, married William M. Craft in 1910. Before her marriage, she was a paid companion to John Bishop's mother, Anna. During the Great Depression, Zilpah started a free lunch program at the local school. She encouraged Anna Bishop to donate a stove. Other community women donated food that Zilpah cooked for the children. (Courtesy of Rosemary Craft.)

W. Robert and Anna B., children of Zilpah B. and William M. Craft, are pictured with a pony. Anna became postmaster in Columbus for many years. W. Robert Craft continued Craft Builders, was on the school board for more than 30 years, was welfare director for Mansfield Township, served as Babe Ruth baseball president, and proudly had the Solar Greenhouse at Northern Burlington County Regional High School named after him. (Courtesy of Rosemary Craft.)

At Wytchwood Gunning Club, Zilpah and William Craft are shown celebrating their 40th anniversary. Guests from left to right are Anna B. Craft, Bill Craft, Zilpah Craft, Elsie Craft, Rosemary Craft, W. Robert Craft, William M. Craft, Emory Craft, Arnie Craft, Dorothy Craft, Carlton Bullock, and David Craft. (Courtesy of Rosemary Craft.)

Located on Atlantic Avenue, the home of Anne Atkinson and George M. Lane was left to them by A. N. Dobbins, owner of the drugstore on the corner. The Lippincott sisters, who owned a hat shop on West Main Street, raised George. Anne Atkinson Lane operated a free public library in the house. (Courtesy of Rosemary Craft.)

Sisters Mary, Anne, Eugenia, and Elsie Lane are standing from left to right in front of their house on Atlantic Avenue. Parents Anne Atkinson and George M. Lane also had two sons, Nathan, an artist, and Peter VanSant, killed in the Philippines in World War II. (Courtesy of Rosemary Craft.)

This farmhouse was built by Nathaniel Burr Atkinson and is now Lynwood Farms development. He also owned the mill in Columbus and the surrounding property. The house became rundown during the Depression and was razed in the early 1950s. He was the grandfather to Anne Atkinson Lane. (Courtesy of Rosemary Craft.)

This stately two-and-a-half-story house on West Main Street was home to the Wills family and later the Thornton family. It was torn down for the Route 206 bypass in 1956. (Courtesy of Tom Sahol.)

Dr. and Mrs. A. B. Peacock of West Main Street hosted the above group of mothers and their children in April 1940 on the first birthday of their daughter Marilyn. From left to right are (first row) Mrs. Everett Johnson, son Robert (in lap), and son Arthur (chair); Mrs. Emmons and daughter Sarah; Mrs. Glenn and daughter Elise; Mrs. Croshaw and daughter Lorraine; Mrs. Townsend and son Eddie; and Mrs. Carslake and son Joseph; (second row) Nancy Cash and sister Dorothy; Mrs. Wills and son Freddie; Mrs. Bryan and daughter Betty; Mrs. Peacock and daughter Marilyn; Mrs. Lloyd Carty and son Ronald; and Mrs. Norman Carty and daughter Janice. (Courtesy of Ronald Carty.)

This Federal-style house, located on the Route 206 ramp into Columbus, originally stood on West Main Street and was relocated when Route 206 was expanded. It was constructed in the late 1700s. Throughout the years, several physicians, including Dr. John Heineken, Dr. A. B. Peacock, and Dr. M. A. Robbins, occupied this home. Marion Girdon, the first treasurer of the Columbus Civic and Athletic Association, occupied this house in 1939. (Courtesy of Mansfield Township Historical Society.)

Edward B. Rockhill (1841–1902) was a direct descendant of the Edward Rockhill who settled in Mansfield Township in 1686. Edward B. and his wife, Annie, raised nine children on a farm on Island Road. The land is now a part of the Goodenough acreage. (Courtesy of Alice Elliott.)

This Rockhill family photograph was taken around 1899. From left to right are (first row) Frank Ingling and Harrison Rockhill; (second row) unidentified, Lucy P. Keeler holding Grace, Annie Rockhill, unidentified, and Edward B. Rockhill; (third row) Mame R. Ingling, Annie Rockhill, Linton Ingling holding Amos, Bertha Rockhill, Rachael R. Clark, Mary Rockhill holding Fred, Walter Clark, and Joseph Rockhill. Missing from this photograph are sons Charles, Edward, and William. (Courtesy of Alice Elliott.)

The Rockhill family had their first-annual reunion in 1946. This picture was taken at the 1950 gathering in Harker's Grove, New Egypt. In 1991, they celebrated the 150th birthday of their patriarch, Edward B. Rockhill at Liberty Lake outside of Columbus. The last reunion was held in 1993. (Courtesy of Alice Elliott.)

This Joseph H. Ingling Sr. family photograph was taken in 1899. From left to right are (first row) Joseph H. Ingling Sr. holding Joseph Jr.; wife, Anna, holding Russell; an unidentified hired helper; and Mattie; (second row) Harvey, Elwood, Bertha, Clarence, Madge, and Addie. (Courtesy of Alice Elliott.)

Content Ingling's wife, Eliza Jane, is shown standing on the front porch of his store, which is attached to the Columbus Inn. Ingling was a painter and confectioner and passed away in 1913. Eliza Jane ran the candy store until her death in 1933. (Courtesy of Alice Elliott.)

This Linton C. Ingling family photograph was taken around 1914. From left to right are (first row) David S., father Linton C. holding Dorothy J., and Ethel B.; (second row) Amos C., Walter F., and mother Mary E. From 1914 to 1920, Linton C. was tax collector. His father, Content, held the same position from 1888 to 1913. (Courtesy of Alice Elliott.)

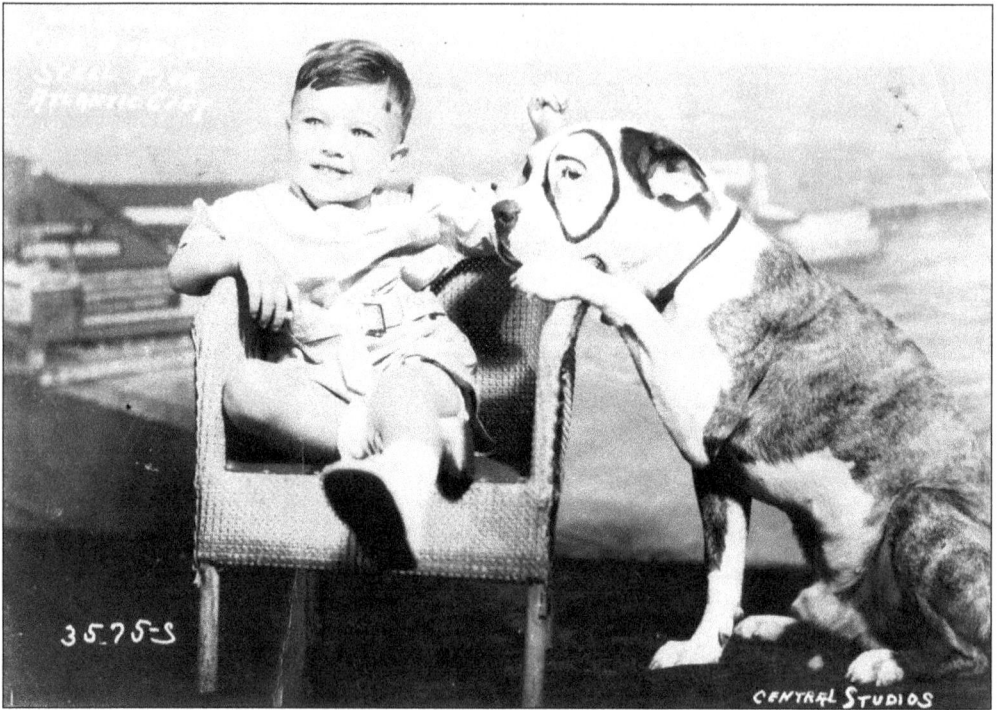

An Ingling grandson, Linton C. Elliott poses with the *Our Gang* dog Pete at the Steel Pier in Atlantic City. (Courtesy of Alice Elliott.)

Joyce Kirby, far left, celebrated her eighth birthday with a party. The guests from left to right are (first row) Barbara Bryan, Barbara Vancza, and Marcy Lippincott; (second row) Eleanor Shreve, Barbara Fisher, Gerrie Shinn, Betty Bryan, and Judy Lippincott; (third row) Janice Lippincott holding baby brother Ray. (Courtesy of Marcy Lippincott.)

This is an aerial view of the intersection of Columbus in the 1940s. Located at the corner of East Main Street and Atlantic Avenue, there was a car dealership, a gas station, and a post office all in one building. The Presbyterian church is behind these buildings on East Main Street. (Courtesy of Donald George.)

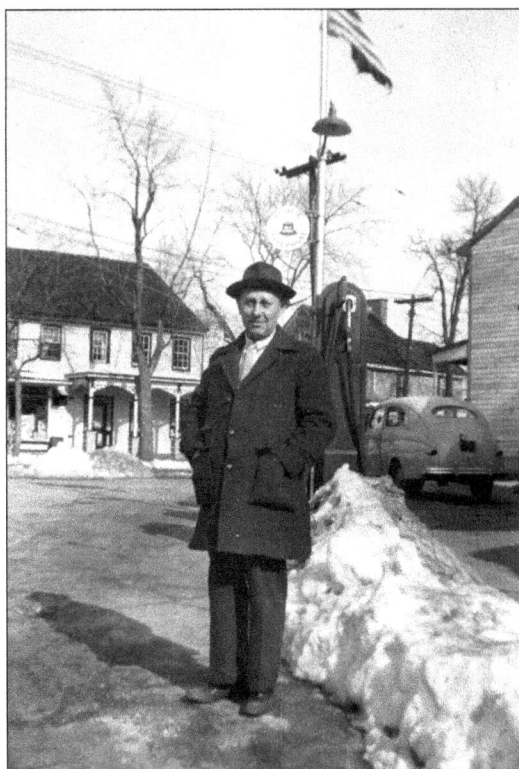

John V. Haskett was the owner of the property at the southeast corner of East Main Street and Atlantic Avenue for over 20 years. He had one of the first televisions in Columbus, and every sports fan in town gathered in the showroom to watch the fights and baseball games. (Courtesy of Jackie Fama.)

Standing on the front porch of the rebuilt Columbus Grange in 1940 are workmen who constructed the Grange hall. Posing from left to right are Emory Craft, Walter Bowne, Robert Townsend, Harry Burr, Roy Carter, Frank Danley, Albert Haines, and Ed Hunt. (Courtesy of Kim Parzyck.)

Lillian Simon is standing in front of the gas station on Route 206 south of Columbus in this 1942 photograph. (Courtesy of Jerry Ingling.)

Young Clifford Townsend sits in the driver's seat of a 1914 Regal car at Yee Auld Columbus Inn Garage, which was on New York Avenue north of the Columbus Inn. Others in the photograph, from left to right, are Floyd Townsend, Harry Heppe, Roy Townsend, and Charles Hankins. (Courtesy of Robert Townsend.)

This house, formerly on Route 206 south of Columbus, was once part of the Shinn farm. (Courtesy of David Potts.)

Built in 1820 in Black Horse (now Columbus), this house was owned by Joseph Bonaparte, Count DeSurvilliers, the former king of Spain and brother to Napoleon Bonaparte. Through a special vote of the state assembly, he was the first noncitizen permitted to own real estate in the state of New Jersey. Bonaparte sold the home to his nephew, Prince Lucien Murat. (Courtesy of John LeRoy Parcels Sr.)

Located on West Main Street, this house was constructed in 1810 by Frank Brognard as a servant's quarters for the Murat house. It later served as a parsonage for the Baptist church. The house is of the same design as the Murat house but on a smaller scale. Dr. Ryland Croshaw, who practiced veterinary medicine in Mansfield Township, owned this home from 1942 to 1990. (Courtesy of John LeRoy Parcels Sr.)

Margaret and Kenneth Landon sit with their children in Siam where Kenneth served as a missionary. Margaret found a diary written by "Anna" and wrote *Anna and the King of Siam*, which was later adapted to the stage play *The King and I*. The Landons lived in Columbus on West Main Street for a time. (Courtesy of Pat Wright.)

This is the Landon house on West Main Street. More recent occupants were Joshua and Dorothy Coulter and family. Joshua was an electrician, and Dorothy coordinated the elementary and high school cafeterias for many years. (Courtesy of Ken Coulter.)

Columbus resident Elwood (Woody) Rossell worked in the Roebling steel plant, as did many other Mansfield Township men. If one did not work on area farms, neighboring foundries in Roebling, Florence, and Burlington provided employment for the local residents. (Courtesy of Jackie Fama.)

Built around 1805 and located on Mount Pleasant Road, this home was occupied throughout the years by the Page family. Members of the Page family served Mansfield Township as its physician, miller, and postmaster. The home was willed to the Hobart family who occupied it until 1979 when the Bassett family bought it at an auction and restored it. (Courtesy of Mildred Bassett.)

The Pine Lawn farmhouse was built in 1849 by Amos Keeler II for his son Amos III. It was located on the acreage where the 300-year-old Keeler Oak is situated. (Courtesy of Marion Pallon.)

This picture was taken in 1898 at the Jake Haines farm on Gaunt's Bridge Road. Shown from left to right are Fred Bryan, Achsala R. Bryan (sitting), Jenny Bryan, George W. Bryan, Mary Ella Bryan, Clement Bryan, and Stockton Bryan. In the carriage are Wilbur E. Bullock, Lillian M. Bryan Bullock, and child Ida Virginia Bullock. (Courtesy of Dorance Wedell.)

Clement Bryan married Jennie Cooper and lived in Georgetown. He then built a home on the corner of Mount Pleasant and Island Roads. (Courtesy of Donna McDowell.)

This picture, taken at the Jake Haines farm near the old Georgetown schoolhouse around 1898, shows a cache of hares from a day of hunting. From left to right are (first row) Stockton Bryan; (second row) Clement Bryan, George Rogers, Wilbur E. Bullock, and George H. Bryan; (third row) George W. Bryan. (Courtesy of Dorance Wedell.)

Shown in this horse-drawn carriage in 1898 are Wilbur E. Bullock, his wife, Lillian M. Bryan Bullock, and their daughter Ida Virginia Bullock. (Courtesy of Dorance Wedell.)

John V. Bishop, owner of Ogston farm on Mount Pleasant Road, stands with one of his prize Jersey cows. (Courtesy of Robert Bishop.)

Ogston farm had one of the finest herds of Jersey cows in the state, and the farm consisted of over 500 acres. John V. Bishop also grew tobacco on about 30 acres, manufacturing a large amount into cigars. (Courtesy of Robert Bishop.)

Ogston farm cows cross Mount Pleasant Road in this picture. The farm occupied many acres on both sides of the road. (Courtesy of Robert Bishop.)

Benjamin Shreve built the Shreve house, located on Mount Pleasant Road, in 1742. Caleb Shreve originally purchased the 325 acres of land in 1699. The Shreve family is well documented in history. Israel, a fourth-generation Shreve, served as a colonel in the American Revolution and knew Gen. George Washington. Shreveport, Louisiana, was named in honor of Israel's son, William. William, also a colonel during the Revolutionary War, had a store at the Mount Pleasant Road homestead, which was burned by the Hessians. (Courtesy of John LeRoy Parcels Sr.)

Located on Mount Pleasant Road, the Crescent Farm was originally a part of the estate of Watson Newbold. This 27-room house may incorporate an earlier house that may have been constructed in the mid-1800s. Daniel D. Van Mater purchased this property from Jacob Ridgeway in 1944. He wanted a farm for his two sons to be able to work when they returned home from World War II. (Courtesy of Dorance Wedell.)

In this picture, from about 1950, Caleb S. Ridgeway stands with his sister Sarah I. Bruce. (Courtesy of Dorance Wedell.)

In this photograph, driver Harvey Wedell stands next to the Locomobile touring car used to chauffeur the Jacob Ridgeway family about 1916, as shown in the license plate. (Courtesy of Dorance Wedell.)

Located on Mount Pleasant Road, this home is known as the Reeder house. The deed to the property dates back to 1782. The house was constructed in 1795 and is listed on an 1876 map as the estate of Watson Newbold. George Sykes resided in this house. He was a member of the Council of Proprietors and represented the Second New Jersey District in Congress from 1843 to 1848. He was a New Jersey assemblyman from 1877 to 1879. The villages of Georgetown and Sykesville are named in his honor. (Courtesy of John LeRoy Parcels Sr.)

Walter Bowne at left and Walter L. Reeder stand in front of the Mansfield Friends Meeting House. (Courtesy of Mansfield Township Historical Society.)

Bowne was a Quaker who lived outside of Columbus on a small farm. He was an interesting man who wrote poetry, drove this old Model T car, and showed up at Grange dinners ready to help where needed. He took the water out of the radiator in freezing weather while he was in the Grange and put it back when he was ready to go home. It was said he liked to dance and was pretty good. Laura Palmer, granddaughter of Reeder, is pictured with Bowne's car. (Courtesy of Mansfield Township Historical Society.)

Barzillai Newbold built the Barzillai Newbold-Bowne house in 1740 for his wife, Sarah Core Newbold. The house is a fine example of a patterned brickwork rural Quaker house of the period. Upon Newbold's death in 1757, he willed the house to his son Thomas Newbold. The house descended in a direct line to the last family owner, Bowne. (Courtesy of Nathan Ewan Archives of Burlington County Library.)

Wanting to become farmers, George and Mary Tutek, with their children, Helen, Mary, George, John, and Annabelle, purchased this home with 120 acres on Georgetown's main street in 1927 from the widow of Dr. Austin H. Patterson, whose office was in the annex to the right. A sixth child, Henry G., was born in 1931. For the latter part of the period of 1847 to 1920, the Georgetown Post Office was in the walk-in basement. (Courtesy of Henry G. Tutek.)

First Lt. Henry G. Tutek, previously an 82nd Airborne Division paratrooper, was commander of the 287th Horse Platoon, the U.S. Army's last cavalry troop. Here in Berlin, Germany, during the cold war in 1956, he prepares to parade. Border patrol and public equestrian competitions with the Germans and American allies were its mission. He later became a lawyer. Older brothers George and John served in the U.S. Navy during World War II. (Courtesy of Henry G. Tutek.)

Henry G. Tutek is shown on a tractor in front of barns on the family farm. (Courtesy of Henry G. Tutek.)

The Applegate house, also known as the Foolstown house, has an interesting history, since the original owner never finished for lack of funds. The town took on the name Foolstown but was renamed Georgetown after George Sykes, who lived on the Reeder farm. In 1765, Thomas Taylor purchased the still-unfinished house. (Courtesy of Nathan Ewan Archives of Burlington County Library.)

Augustus Montrey Sr., a member of one of the first families in Georgetown, owned a wagon building and horseshoing business, established in 1884. (Courtesy of Roy Hendrickson.)

Augustus Montrey Jr. and Gladys Montrey owned an appliance store, gas station, and general store in Georgetown for many years. They also had an appliance store in Columbus for five years. Gladys Montrey was very involved with the Columbus Grange as the juvenile matron and was instrumental in bringing the state police to Mansfield. (Courtesy of William Montrey.)

Caleb Newbold constructed this house in 1764 for his wife Mary Foster Newbold. It is located on the Georgetown-Wrightstown Road, Route 545. The home remained in the possession of the Newbold family for more than 100 years. It is recorded as being owned by W. Newbold in 1876. The Newbolds were a prominent family of Quakers who settled much of northern Burlington County. (Courtesy of Nathan Ewan Archives of Burlington County Library.)

Israel Kirby owned Homestead Farm, located on Route 68, in 1878. Benjamin and Anna Kirby were the next generation, and then Raymond and Mildred bought it in 1931. This aerial shot was taken in 1948 or 1949. (Courtesy of Alfred Kirby.)

Thought to be the first department store in New Jersey, the Georgetown Store was probably built around 1850. The store partners were Nathan Wright Frazer and Samuel Johnson. It was the first store in the area to have gaslights, and rumor has it that the building had an elevator. People came from Philadelphia to buy furs here. Newbold Hutchinson demolished the building in the 1950s or 1960s. (Courtesy of the Collection of the Burlington County Historical Society.)

In this 1938 photograph, Betty Montrey and Ruth Carslake man the gas pumps at the Esso gas station in Georgetown. (Courtesy of William Montrey.)

The Aaronson homestead was located north of Columbus on Route 206. The Aaronson ladies and children are dressed in their finery for a special occasion. (Courtesy of Janet Aaronson.)

George Aaronson Sr. and his wife, Edith Miller Aaronson, pose with their sons George "Bud" (left) and William (right) outside their farmhouse. Four generations of the Aaronsons raised their families on the farm. They grew crops of corn and soybeans and raised Guernsey cows. (Courtesy of Janet Aaronson.)

Carlton Alloway served in the Marines in World War II. He was killed in action. (Courtesy of Elizabeth Alloway.)

The Alloway family were farmers on what is now called Public Road. Elizabeth and John, shown in the back of this photograph, continued to operate the farm until the 1990s. (Courtesy of Elizabeth Alloway.)

Elijah Alloway, brother to Carlton, served in the navy in World War II. (Courtesy of Elizabeth Alloway.)

Henry Reeves (left) of Brookdale farm and Charles Howard of Sunny Lane farm enjoyed a lifelong friendship. Both men were engaged in dairy farming and doing custom farmwork. (Courtesy of Hank Reeves.)

This house was built in the mid-1800s. It is located just one-eighth of a mile west of the intersection of Hedding Road and Route 206. Caleb Wood has been identified as the original owner. He was a farmer and breeder of Jersey cattle. The property later came under the ownership of the Tallman family and then the Albanese family. (Courtesy of Marion Tallon.)

In 1914, this farmhouse sat on the 165-acre Ephriam Dull farm that was located at the top of the hill on Hedding Road across from the Tallman farm. The house is now gone. (Courtesy of David Potts.)

The family of Joseph Forgan sits on the front porch of their farmhouse in 1911. Shown from left to right are Mary, Carl Jr., Irene, Joseph Sr., and Anna. The house was built in the 1700s, and the farm consisted of 90 acres. (Courtesy of Elsie Forgan.)

The Forgan family bought the farm on the Jobstown and Bordentown Road (now named North Island Road) in 1900. In this 1911 photograph, the barns of the dairy farm are shown. When Mary Forgan died in 1920, the farm was sold, but her husband, Joseph Sr., still held the mortgage. In 1934, Carl Forgan Jr. repurchased the farm, and it is still in the family to this date. (Courtesy of Elsie Forgan.)

This is an aerial view of the Roger Kirby farm from the back. Kirby was the pilot of the plane while John Townsend took the photographs around 1939. Located on Old York Road east of Hedding, the dairy farm was 145 acres at one time. (Courtesy of Alfred Kirby.)

The Kirby family poses for this studio portrait about 1916. Father Benjamin Kirby and mother Anna are with their children, from left to right, Raymond, Edna, and Roger. (Courtesy of Alfred Kirby.)

This aerial view of the Royal Kinsley farm on Hedding Road, which occupies 130 acres, shows many barns and outbuildings that no longer exist. Rueben Greenberg bought the farm from Kinsley, and a previous owner was Ambrose Wainwright, son of Charles W. Wainwright. (Courtesy of Alfred Kirby.)

Located between the bank of the Delaware River and Burlington Road (Route 130), this house, known as Mount Hope, was built for William Biddle in 1684. William Biddle was one of the wealthiest and most influential men in West Jersey. He was a judge of the county courts and became a member of the Council of Proprietors of West New Jersey about 1695. The New Jersey governor selected him as one of his council. (Courtesy of Nathan Ewan Archives of Burlington County Library.)

Joseph and Rose (Bogdanyi) Lukacs pose for this formal portrait with their children, Elsie, Elizabeth, Pearl, Joseph, and Rose, in 1928. (Courtesy of Rose Volcskai.)

The Bogdanyi/Lukacs farmstead lies on Old York Road east of Hedding, where Joseph and Rose raised their children. Rose and Stephen Volcskai bought the nearby house on the corner in 1955. (Courtesy of Rose Volcskai.)

Children in the hamlet of Hedding line up for this picture in 1917. Posing from left to right are Margie Rossell, Paul Walder, Raymond Rossell, Charles Walder, Libby Rossell, Magdaline Walder, and Emmaline Nixon. (Courtesy of Claudia Teal.)

Hedding-area teenagers are enjoying a day out in 1920. From left to right are (first row) Hobart Shreve, Grace Nixon, Malcolm Willits, and Harry Willits; (second row) Beulah Willits, Elsie McCalahis, and Edith Nixon. (Courtesy of Claudia Teal.)

The Hedding United Methodist Church, located on the northwest corner of the main intersection in Hedding, was constructed in 1847. At this time, John Biddle gave a plot of ground to the church. Previous to this date, services were held in a schoolhouse on the property. This was the first school in Hedding. The hamlet's name, Three Tuns, was changed in 1849 to honor Bishop Elijah Hedding of the Methodist Church. (Courtesy of Ron Asson.)

The village of Three Tuns is located on Old York Road and Hedding-Kinkora Road. At the dawn of the 20th century, a general store called Page's store and a residence sat at the southwest corner. (Courtesy of Ron Asson.)

On the southeast corner, Three Tuns had a wheelwright shop, owned by Asa Carty, who manufactured wagons and carriages. Three Tuns also contained two blacksmith shops. (Courtesy of Ron Asson.)

The Three Tuns Tavern, for which the town was named in the 18th century, had a sign depicting three casks, or tuns, intended to attract the thirsty traveler. After a succession of tavern keepers through the 19th century, the tavern was razed by John Shreve and replaced with a new residence and general store. (Courtesy of Ron Asson.)

Charles W. Wainwright, father to William Henry Wainwright, was born in 1836 in Three Tuns where he and his family worked the farm Old Homestead. He bought the property from his elders and died in 1908. (Courtesy of Carl Wainwright.)

Pictured in the wagon is William Henry Wainwright in front of the house on the Old Homestead farm around 1900. The farm is in its seventh generation of the family and consists of 240 acres that sits northwest of Hedding. (Courtesy of Curtis Wainwright.)

The infant Charles Raymond Wainwright, born in 1925, sits for this professional portrait. He is the grandson of William Henry Wainwright and was born on the family farm, of which he and his wife, Betty Pigott Wainwright, bought from his parents in 1950. Charles and Betty raised their six children, Charles II, Cynthia, Claudia, Connie, Curtis, and Carl, on the farm of which Curtis continues to farm. (Courtesy of Betty Pigott Wainwright.)

The oldest child of Charles and Emmaline Pigott, Betty Pigott sits in her carriage on the family's front porch in Hedding. The Hedding School can be seen in the background of the photograph. (Courtesy of Betty Pigott Wainwright.)

The John B. Shreve General Store replaced the Three Tuns Tavern in 1915 when John and Maude Shreve purchased the property. They operated the general store until the 1940s, and their son Hobart continued to live here until his death in 1990. (Courtesy of Claudia Teal.)

This brick farmhouse was the home of the Pray family on Kinkora Road. The family owned a large tract of farmland north of Hedding and also had many greenhouses across the road. The house is now stucco covered and lovingly restored. (Courtesy of John Main.)

This view of Kinkora Road looking south from Route 25 (Route 130 today) is during a winter snow. (Courtesy of Claudia Teal.)

It was at the Kinkora station that Charles G. Roebling, founder of the village of Roebling and the Roebling Plant, and Jacob Hoffer met for the first time. In 1905, Roebling paid Hoffer $17,000 for 115 acres and developed the homes for the workers and the wire rope plant. (Courtesy of Lou Borbi.)

The Columbus and Kinkora Railroad was incorporated in 1866. In 1871, terminals extended from Kinkora to Lisbon. In November 1906, it was recorded that the Camden and Amboy Railroad Company was operating a railroad in Mansfield Township. The route ran along Railroad Avenue, the length of Mill Lane, and into Kinkora. During World War II, the train carried servicemen from Kinkora to Camp Dix. Trains traveled the railroad to Trenton, Philadelphia, and New York. Passengers often changed trains at Kinkora. (Courtesy of Richard Szatkowski.)

The Kinkora General Store was located on the Delaware River side (west) of Route 130, just opposite Hedding (Kinkora) Road. It was situated near the Kinkora railroad station just behind the Jacob Lee Winery. The store sold "groceries and provisions." It was in business during the years when Kinkora was the bustling commercial hub of Mansfield Township, from the mid-1850s to the early 1900s. (Courtesy of Mansfield Township Historical Society.)

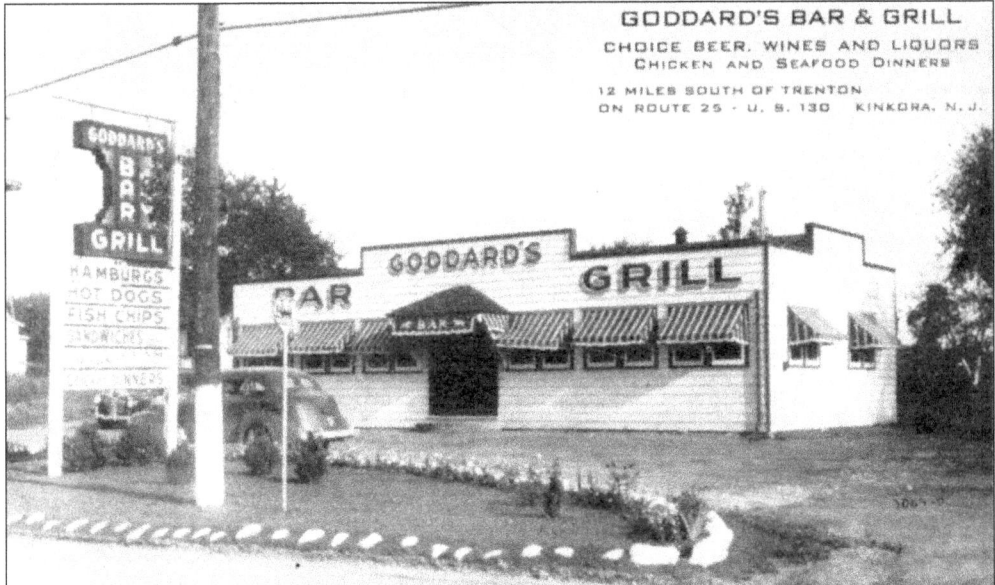

Built in 1937 by Orvil Goddard Sr., this establishment, located on Route 130 north, was known throughout the community for the fine chicken and seafood meals that were served. (Courtesy of Lois Reeves.)

The gang from the Kinkora Garage, from left to right, includes Jimmie McCay, Lewis Comp, and Charles Dubell. (Courtesy of Alice Elliott.)

The front yard of Mary Steiner, shown here with her daughter Mary Borbi (right), is abloom with tall mums that she grew for her great-grandchildren to sell to passing motorists along Route 25 (Route 130 today) at Kinkora. The price for a medium bundle was 15¢, and a large bundle was 25¢ in 1950. (Courtesy of Lou Borbi.)

On the northern side of Mansfield Road west is the Revonah farm. The house, known as the W. Biddle house, was constructed in the late 1700s. It is an excellent example of a Federal-style farmhouse. Some outbuildings may also date back to the late 1700s. Purchased by William Potts in 1902, the farm was sold to William's son Bill, who kept it until 1963, when it was sold to Norman Goldman. (Courtesy of Mansfield Township Historical Society.)

The oldest sons of William and Anna Potts pose for a photographer. Frank (left), born in 1892, was a mason who lived in Columbus. Austin was born in 1888. (Courtesy of Mansfield Township Historical Society.)

William (Bill) Potts (left), born in 1898, is seen in this photograph with sister Mabel, who was two years older. Bill bought the Revonah farm from his father. (Courtesy of Roy Hendrickson.)

Stella Potts (left) born in 1901 and Rena (right), born in 1907, were the youngest children of William and Anna Potts. (Courtesy of Roy Hendrickson.)

Brothers Harold and Larry Potts are fishing off the bridge of Spring Hill Brook on Axe Factory Road in the late 1930s. Harold and his other brother Alvin ran a dairy farm on Axe Factory Road, and Alvin was well known for his custom carpentry, especially his grandfather clocks. (Courtesy of David Potts.)

Raymond Tucci was a hired hand for the farm of Leonard and Alice Potts in the 1920s. (Courtesy of David Potts.)

Sarah Ridgeway Potts grew up in Mansfield Township and married Thomas Potts. They resided on Columbus Road in Florence Township, raising two children, William Gaskill and Mary. Sarah died in 1871, as seen on her funeral notice. (Courtesy of Dorothy Potts Bowers.)

Yourself and family are respect-fully invited to attend the funeral of

SARAH R. POTTS.

From the residence of her husband, Thomas Potts, on Columbus road, near Burlington, on Monday, the 4th instant, at 12 o'clock, M.

BURLINGTON, Dec. 2, 1871.

The Spahr family of Shady Lane farm on Mill Lane is seen in this 1945 photograph. Albert Spahr Sr. and Albert Spahr Jr. are holding the horses while grandmom and grandpop Berringer, Evelyn Berringer, and assorted Berringer and Spahr children pose for the photographer. (Courtesy of Kim Parzyck.)

The Walder family operated a dairy farm on Mill Lane, once owned by one of Mansfield's early settlers, Thomas Scattergood. The farm consisted of 183 acres and occupied both sides of the railroad that ran along Mill Lane. Charles Walder (right) owned the farm from 1943 and farmed until his death in 1975. (Courtesy of Marion Reeves.)

Shown from left to right, three of the children of Charles and Sarah Walder, Darlene, Charles, and Marion, pose patiently for this 1935 photograph. (Courtesy of Marion Reeves.)

The Barclay Townsend farm is shown looking south on Petticoat Bridge Road. It was sold in 1924. The barns are gone but the house still stands. (Courtesy of Robert Townsend.)

The Colkitt farm is shown in this photograph from about 1905. Benjamin Colkitt bought the farm, located on Petticoat Bridge Road, in 1862, but when his two sons died of typhoid fever, it was thought that the disease was contracted from the nearby creek, so he traded the property with Joseph Colkitt of Arneytown for his property. It remained in this Colkitt family until the Gilberts bought it in 1970. The photograph shows young Everett Colkitt in the field with his parents by the carriage. Isiah Goldy built this brick farmhouse in 1812 on the site of the 1776 skirmish between Colonial and Hessian troops. (Courtesy of Nancy Gilbert.)

Originally the John Sutton farm in 1919, this 142-acre farm was bought by Fred Wainwright Sr. in 1946. It straddled Mansfield and Florence Townships on Florence-Columbus Road. Fred Wainwright Jr. bought the farm from his father in 1972 and ran a successful dairy business with his sons. (Courtesy of Fred Wainwright Jr.)

From left to right, seed salesman John Staedle talks with Fred Wainwright Sr. and sons Fred "Fritz" Wainwright Jr. and Ted Wainwright. (Courtesy of Fred Wainwright Jr.)

In 1948, Carl and Charlotte Huebler built a home on the Columbus Road where they raised their three children, Jean (Wainwright), Carl, and Mildred (Powell). Both Carl Sr. and Charlotte were avid gardeners. Passersby enjoyed the large plot of colorful blooms that graced their property each growing season. (Courtesy of Jean Wainwright.)

Thomas Scattergood, Mansfield's first settler, owned the tract of land on which this house stands. Caleb Scattergood, a descendant of Thomas Scattergood, constructed the house in 1808. It is located on Jacksonville-Hedding Road on a hill that overlooks Crafts Creek. Hartley and Elizabeth Stevenson purchased this property in 1925 from the Wright family and operated a dairy farm here. (Courtesy of Marion Tallon.)

This farm was on the Columbus-Florence Road before Interstate 295 was built. Frank Wainwright bought it in 1901 and then son Harold and grandson Franklin Wainwright operated it until 1956. The farm was then sold to William Wainwright and continued operation until Interstate 295 came through. (Courtesy of Fred Wainwright Jr.)

Pictured is Franklin Wainwright (right) with a visiting soldier from Fort Dix in 1943. The Florence Methodist Church brought soldiers from Fort Dix for Sunday afternoon breaks. Some of the men visited local farms. (Courtesy of Franklin Wainwright.)

Two

EDUCATION
AND WORSHIP

Originally located behind the brick Friends Meeting House on Route 206, this frame schoolhouse was eventually moved closer to Route 206. It served as a school between the late 1800s and early 1900s. Elizabeth Bowne taught 48 students in this school. A teacher in the early 1900s was Mabel Taylor Bullock, wife of Dr. Bullock who practiced medicine in Columbus for many years. (Courtesy of the Collection of the Burlington County Historical Society.)

Approved for the "promotion of learning" on April 16, 1846, a number of prominent Mansfield citizens created a capital stock of $4,000 for the Columbus Seminary Association. In 1869, the land was sold to Lodge No. 101 of the Independent Order of Odd Fellows (IOOF). In 1870, the Columbus Seminary Association, under president William Kirkbride, was started. Prof. L. N. Prentice assumed leadership of the seminary in 1885. The building was sold in 1940 to Bordentown Lodge No. 16 of the IOOF. (Courtesy of Ethel Townsend.)

Originally located on Gaunts Bridge Road, this school building at one time sat on the southern tip of the triangle that is formed by the Georgetown and Jobstown Roads. A map dated 1849 shows that this school was in use at that time. In 1914, it was moved to the Charles Burtis farm and used for the storage of corn. In 1976, the building was given to the Mansfield Township Historical Society for renovation. It is currently located north of Columbus on Route 206 at the civic club recreation field. (Courtesy of Mansfield Township Historical Society.)

Located on Locust Street in Columbus, this school was constructed in 1883. It consisted of one large room downstairs and one large room upstairs. In each room, one teacher taught four grades. The first two years of high school were taught in this building. Students wishing to complete high school attended a nearby school for their final two years. The Locust Street School was closed in 1914. (Courtesy of Mansfield Township Historical Society.)

This is a picture of 26 girls, 19 boys, and a teacher at the Locust Street School in Columbus. The building is now known as the Craft Apartments. The only identified student is Effie Fennimore, left of the teacher in the first row. She later married Joseph Armstrong and is mother to Russell and Roland Armstrong. (Courtesy of Mansfield Township Historical Society.)

Columbus schoolteachers pose for this 1919 picture. Mabel Harvey is one of the teachers. (Courtesy of Alice Elliott.)

Children pose for this 1912 school picture behind the Mansfield Friends Meeting House. Some of the children include twins Florence and Margaret Bradley, Amy Moore, Carl Forgan, Edyth Pope, Carl Pope, and Ted Kirby. (Courtesy of Elsie Forgan.)

The Three Tuns School was a wood structure behind the Methodist church and had one teacher. Pictured from left to right are (first row) Clifford Shreve, Bertie Wainwright, Myra Wainwright, Bess Malsbury, teacher Minnie Kreder, Grace Nixon, unidentified, Eva Aaronson, Edith Nixon, unidentified, and Ed Aaronson; (second row) Sarah Poinsett, Mabel Kinsley, Florence Nixon, Grace Wainwright, and two unidentified girls; (third row) Warner Wainwright, three unidentified boys, Raymond Carty, Morris Horn, Charles Blake, and Charles Malsbury. (Courtesy of Claudia Teal.)

After closing the Three Tuns School in 1914 when the township built four new brick schools, the building was used by the church as a hall. Pictured from left to right are (first row) Hobart Shreve, Ralph Malsbury, Stanley Carty, Clifford Shreve, unidentified, and William Potts; (second row) all seven unidentified; (third row) Stella Potts, unidentified, Thomas Ettinger, unidentified, unidentified, Margaret Green, Edith Carty, Helen Nixon, Ella Aaronson, unidentified, and the unidentified teacher; (fourth row) Myra Wainwright, Mabel Potts, Reba Ettinger, Helen Carty, Bertie Wainwright, and Bessie Malsbury. (Courtesy of Claudia Teal.)

The two-room brick Hedding School in 1914 was located on Old York Road. Pictured from left to right are (first row) Lenora Olah, Sylvia Epstein, Dorothy Middleton, Sara Kimble, May Kimble, Bernice Giberson, Elizabeth Rambo, and Magdalena Walder; (second row) Rena Potts, Emmaline Nixon, Mae Epstein, and unidentified; (third row) Alfreda Dubell, Isadore Greenberg, Jacob Greenberg, Roland Armstrong, Kenneth Kreder, Pierce Pray, George Olah, Russell Roberts, and Verna Aaronson; (fourth row) teacher Millicent Weeks. (Courtesy of Claudia Teal.)

In this 1926 school picture, grades four through seven line up with the Shreve house in the background. Pictured from left to right are (first row) Paul Bendage, Jim McCay, George Barrett, Dan Hay, Frank Bear, Roger Dubell, John Bear, Joe Walder, Wilmer Carty, John Jaichner, and Mike Lishora; (second row) Norman Carty, Russell Armstrong, Paul Walder, Lawrence Pray, Charles Barrett, Lloyd Carty, Leon Rossell, Steve Bear, Casper Malsbury, Horace Lloyd, and Aaron Pulmutter; (third row) Lillian Marsh, Anna Bendage, Grace Armstrong, Doris Roberts, Lucy Barrett, Mary Sigket, teacher Alice Engle, Ethel Bogdon, Melanie Jaichner, Margie Rossell, Susie Marsh, and Alice Carty. (Courtesy of Claudia Teal.)

The younger classes of Hedding School in the 1930s are dressed for a Native American play. Teacher Millicent Weeks lived with the McKenzie family in Hedding. Pictured from left to right are (first row) Anna Schiff, Barbara Cliver, Jeannette Roberts, Shirley Bender, Doris Wainwright, Eleanor Daly, Kathy Kirby, and Betty Pigott; (second row) Dorothy Emlen, Gloria McKenzie, Helen Schiff, Alice Jaichner, Alice Asay, Holmes Hay, Herb Zelley, and Lois McKenzie; (third row) Bill Pigott, Joe Nemeth, Rufus Daly, Paul Odri, and Harold Potts. (Courtesy of Laura Potts.)

The older classes of the Hedding School performed a play about Egypt with Ruth Wainwright dressed as a mummy. Her older brother Charles is at left on the second row. Mrs. Mankey, the teacher, came to work every day from Haddonfield and never missed a day, no matter what the weather was like. (Courtesy of David Potts.)

Schoolchildren from the Hedding School in 1939, from left to right, are (first row) Larry Potts, Cliff Hay, Edith Johnson, Ruth Johnson, unidentified, Shirley Bender, Doris Wainwright, Lois Jaichner, June Emlen, and Ray Walders; (second row) Anne Schiff, Alex Schiff, unidentified, unidentified, Holmes Hay, Jeanette Roberts, Barbara Cliver, and Paul Walder. (Courtesy of Lois Reeves.)

Located across the street from the Locust Street schoolhouse, Columbus School was the largest of four brick schools built in Mansfield Township in 1914. Initially it was a two-room structure. Throughout the decades of the 1930s through the 1960s, classrooms were added to this structure to accommodate the educational needs of Mansfield's children. This school educated Mansfield children from kindergarten through grade eight until the 1960s. At this time, the Northern Burlington County Regional School District was formed, and Mansfield's seventh and eighth graders as well as its high school students were educated in this new facility. (Courtesy of Tom Sahol.)

This is a picture of the third-grade class of Columbus School in 1920. Pictured from left to right are (first row) Les Walwyn, Arthur Gilbert, Arthur Poinsett, Norman Hall, David Ingling, Dick Perkins, Howard Gilbert, and Ed Shaedle; (second row) Helen Asay Wainwright, Anna Ritter, Martha Horner, Dorothy Ingling Elliott, Edith Craft, Della Stacko, Gladys Foulks, Sarah Perkins, Elizabeth Stackhouse, Evelyn Taylor, Anna Hall, Sarah Straw, unidentified, unidentified, Molly Guse Poddlack, and Thelma Bishop; (third row) Bill Smith, Frank Tallman, Truman Wright, teacher Mrs. Gaskill, Ernest Ingling, Irving Tallman, Anna Lincoln, Janet Angle, Violet Burtis Shinn, and Anna Craft. (Courtesy of Alice Elliott.)

Students from the seventh-grade class at Columbus School are pictured in front of the school in the early 1920s. (Courtesy of Alfred Kirby.)

Shown are students from Columbus School. From left to right are (first row) Myrtle Archer, Leon Russell, Ruth Stevens, Ray Auer, Victor Vancza, and Elizabeth Stackhouse; (second row) Elizabeth Meadows, Alice Carty, Dot Kirby, Charles Barrett, Norman Carty, Ada Potts, Melanie Jaichner,

and Susie Marsh; (third row) Edward Shaedle, Libbie Schaedle, Marguerite Ridgeway, Madge Koenig, Robert Scattergood, Russell Armstrong, and Howard Day. Two of the schoolchildren would not have their pictures taken. (Courtesy of Mansfield Township Historical Society.)

This is the eighth-grade graduating class of Columbus School in 1937, with teachers Alva Pray and Mrs. Creamer standing at each end of the second row. (Courtesy of Jackie Fama.)

This is Mrs. Creamer's Columbus School class in 1941. Some of the students included Eleanor Stanton, Helen Archer, Marilyn Tallman, Joy Ann Jastrow, Alice Davenport, Horace Lippincott, Russell Archer, Joe Suydan, Irvin Adams, Don Kennedy, Linton Elliott, Henry Tutek, Walter Gower, Maurice Stevenson, William Koenig, Bob Shinn, Dorance Wedell, Ed Powell, Ed Gilbert, and Ralph Archer. (Courtesy of Alice Elliott.)

Lois Jaichner and George Aaronson attended the 1949 senior ball at Bordentown High School. (Courtesy of Hank Reeves.)

This is a picture of eighth-grade graduates in 1951 at the Columbus Grange. Posing from left to right are (first row) Alyce Lippincott, Jeanette Richardson, Shirley Foster, Alice Ingling, Ruth Heitman, Jane Horner, Alice Elliott, Janet Conrey, Joyce Kirby, Emily Mangin, Marion Pigott, Barbara Bryan, and Joan Hannah; (second row) Harry George, Irving Carslake, Mike Hatala, Arthur Forsman, Arthur Bagley, Wilmont Johnson, David Broderick, Paul Hanisch, Kenneth Coulter, David Reed, and teacher Mrs. Richardson. (Courtesy of Alice Elliott.)

Shown sitting on the Harley in front of the Bordentown High School in 1952 are Herb Gower (left) and Sonny Armstrong. Standing behind from left to right are Cliff Hay, Bob Townsend, Harry Lavell, and Jack Soden. (Courtesy of Hank Reeves.)

Ilene Sheedy's third-grade class at the Columbus School in 1959 is pictured in their classroom. Shown from left to right are (first row) Wally Kerlin, Steve Romine, Bill Phares, and Barbara Haluska; (second row) Joseph Olynk, Arlene Verog, unidentified, and Bill Murphy; (third row) Norman Hopkins, Ronald Orban, Donna Ingling, and Linda Haluska; (fourth row) Bob Tallon, Thomas Kaufman, unidentified, and Charles Wainwright II; (fifth row) Donna Reeves, Tim Tettemer, Shirley Greenway, and Ann Forgan; (sixth row) Dorothy Marias, Carl Davison, Anna Mae Locke, and Bobby Davison; (seventh row) Paul Someruck, Patty Romine, Shirley Johnson, and Frank Parkison; (eighth row) Ned Parker, Glen Reed, Sheedy, Benny Giberson, and Kenny Beebe. (Courtesy of Bob Tallon.)

Mansfield Meeting House,
Columbus, N. J.

This brick Quaker meetinghouse, located on Route 206 just southwest of the intersection with Georgetown Road, was constructed in 1812. It replaced a frame structure that was built in 1731 and destroyed by fire. Quakers settled Mansfield Township, and in the early years this structure was the hub of activity for Quakers residing in and near the hamlet of Mansfield Square. It was the activities centered in this structure that first brought recognition to Mansfield Township. (Courtesy of Alfred Kirby.)

St. Lukes Episcopal Church,
Columbus, N. J.

Early records indicate that St. Luke's Episcopal Church was in existence on West Main Street in 1875. The Reverend Riley of the Burlington Military College led the congregation in 1885. Some members were Anna Page, Mrs. Israel Kerlin, Miriam Crispin, Irene Potts, Esther Hewitt, Amelia Minnick Cobb, and Mrs. George Black. The church was demolished to make room for a ramp that leads from Route 206 into Columbus. (Courtesy of Mansfield Township Historical Society.)

95

The Columbus Baptist Church, located on West Main Street, was dedicated in 1873. The Columbus Baptist congregation in Mansfield met as early as 1830 in an old carpenter's shop. In 1839, a church edifice was erected where services were held until 1872, when it was sold to the Mansfield Township governing body to be used as a town hall on Pine Street, now Atlantic Avenue. Prior to the construction of the 1873 edifice, baptisms were held in Crafts Creek near the Columbus Civic and Athletic Association building. (Courtesy of Columbus Baptist Church.)

Taken August 1, 1937, this picture shows members of the congregation of the Columbus Baptist Church. Shown are Sarah Ruth Davis, pastor Milbor Davis, Anna Haines, Clara Belle Townsend, Harry Newell, Anna Ridgeway, Joseph Ridgeway, and Roy Townsend. (Courtesy of Columbus Baptist Church.)

A fishing trip was sponsored by Roy Townsend for Baptist men. They pose here in front of Stevenson Lumber Yard with their catch on August 20, 1936. Shown from left to right are (first row) unidentified, John Alloway, Carl Alloway (died serving in the Marines in World War II), Warren Townsend, Eddie Lippincott, unidentified, and Elijah Alloway; (second row) Roy Townsend, Borden Shinn, Jack Wedell, Bob Craft, Harry Titus, Ronald Shinn, Henry Nutt, Ed Bradley, Joe Nutt, Arthur Nutt Jr. (died serving in the navy in World War II), and Arthur Nutt Sr. (Courtesy of Columbus Baptist Church.)

The congregation of the Methodist Episcopal Church met at the Black Horse School; their first building was purchased in 1814, and they converted it into a church in 1849. It was later sold and moved to the south side of East Main Street and used as a "molasses house." Pictured here is the second Wesley Methodist Church, which was erected in 1857 at a cost of about $1,000. (Courtesy of Wesley Methodist Church.)

The present structure was built in 1907 at a cost of $9,500 and designed by Phineas Smith. In 1907, the Wesley Methodist Episcopal Church was incorporated, and in 1920, the mortgage was burned. (Courtesy of Wesley Methodist Church.)

The choir gathers on the front porch of the Hedding United Methodist Church on Palm Sunday in 1948. Pictured from left to right are (first row) Reba Parker, Alice Jaichner, Lois Jaichner, Shirley Bender, and Doris Wainwright; (second row) Merle Carty, Jeanette Roberts, Joan Dengler, and Pauline Barton; (third row) Ruth Wainwright, Holmes Hay, Harold Potts, and Betty Pigott; (fourth row) Kenneth Parks, Ronald Asson, William Pigott, and Herbert Zelly. (Courtesy of Ronald Asson.)

Just married, Marion (Walder) and Robert Reeves leave the church with family and friends surrounding them on June 3, 1950. In the background are the south corners of Old York Road and Hedding Road. (Courtesy of Marion Reeves.)

The earliest meetings of the First Presbyterian Church of Columbus were held under some large trees as early as 1825. It was officially organized in 1835 and incorporated in 1879. In 1882, W. O. Wilson of Burlington was contracted to build the 46-by-20-foot structure on East Main Street. Some early pastors were H. Hall, S. Miller, and G. S. Schuler, who wrote the popular hymn "Make Me a Blessing." The church was demolished in the late 1970s. (Courtesy of Alfred Kirby.)

The education building was built behind the church sanctuary, encasing an earlier addition. Then the old structure was demolished in 1956. That new building is now the Mansfield Township Municipal Complex, and the sanctuary was torn down. (Courtesy of Pat Wright.)

Three

ORGANIZATIONS AND CLUBS

The Franklin Fire Engine Company was organized about 1828 and reorganized in 1861. The firehouse was located on Atlantic Avenue next to the town hall. Charles Carslake, shown in the above photograph, drives the Martin fire engine in 1914. The vehicle had solid rubber tires, a chain-drive engine, and chemical tanks. (Courtesy of Janet Aaronson.)

A 65-foot bell tower was erected next to the firehouse, but the original firehouse in this 1914 photograph had a bell on top of the building. The all-volunteer membership shown here are most likely grandfathers of present-day members. (Courtesy of Franklin Fire Company.)

Members of the Franklin Fire Company pose for a special occasion such as a convention. The firehouse was moved back and expanded when Atlantic Avenue was widened to accommodate Route 206 traffic through town. (Courtesy of Franklin Fire Company.)

Covering 23 square miles, Franklin Fire Company members pose in 1936 with their 1935 Ford pumper, which is still in the township, and the 1930 Ford pumper. Some members were Roger Kirby, Goldy Bryan, Edward Shinn, Robert Craft, David Ingling, Wilmer Carty, Robert Townsend, Charles DuBell, Roland Armstrong, and Sy DuBell. (Courtesy of Franklin Fire Company.)

Shown from left to right are Dick Archer, Art Taylor, and Earl Hopkins accepting keys to a new 1970 Hahn pumper from Mayor Bill Aaronson and committeemen Wilmer Carty and John Berezcki. (Courtesy of Franklin Fire Company.)

Located on the east side of Atlantic Avenue, this building served as the Mansfield Township Municipal Building in 1872. This was originally the Columbus Baptist Church grounds. The building was constructed in 1839 and sold to the township in 1872. The jail cellar was constructed in 1873. (Courtesy of Mansfield Township Historical Society.)

This picture shows Sheriff William Townsend's clambake in Mansfield. He was elected sheriff of Burlington County and officiated at the last hanging in Mount Holly, for which invitations were sent out. Townsend also founded with a partner the Townsend and Ware Coal and Feed business in 1900. Townsend died in 1926. (Courtesy of Mansfield Township Historical Society.)

The original Columbus Grange No. 58, located on Atlantic Avenue, was the social center of the community in addition to cooperative buying of coal, seed, sundries, and other items for farmers. Farmers and their families gathered here for meetings, education, dinners, and entertainment. At its height, the membership was well over 300. The grange was organized in 1874, but the hall was built in 1910. (Courtesy of Mansfield Township Historical Society.)

Members of the Columbus Grange presented this pageant of the Flora Court at the state Grange convention in the early 1900s. (Courtesy of Columbus Grange No. 58.)

The second floor of the Columbus Grange was a meeting room. The women sat on one side, and the men sat on the other, with office stations at various points in the room. The meetings and ceremonies are based on Masonic rituals. Two monthly meetings were held with covered-dish suppers beforehand. (Courtesy of Mansfield Township Historical Society.)

This picture shows what remains of the original Columbus Grange Hall after an arsonist set the building ablaze on December 28, 1938. The entire second floor was completely burned. Edwin Shinn, master at that time, held meetings at the township hall for two years while the new hall was being built. (Courtesy of Robert Townsend.)

The newly rebuilt Columbus Grange Hall was dedicated in 1940. The hall had to be rebuilt after an arson spree in 1938 destroyed the original Grange hall as well as a few other structures. The Grange is still active today but with a much smaller membership than in previous years. (Courtesy of Columbus Grange No. 58.)

This photograph shows the Grange hall stage backdrop mural painted by Nathan Lane, a local artist, depicting area businesses. The Home Economics Committee sold advertising space to raise funds to pay for the hall rebuilding. The approximate cost of the new building was $15,000 and in May 1946, a "burning of the mortgage" ceremony was held. (Courtesy of Columbus Grange No. 58.)

As with all Granges in New Jersey, Columbus Grange created elaborate exhibits with local produce at the state farm fairs. (Courtesy of Columbus Grange No. 58.)

Gladys Montrey of Georgetown, shown in the third row, was the juvenile grange matron from 1938 to 1953. The local children who participated, from left to right, are (first row) Jack Fleuer, Shirley Shinn, Joan Rockhill, Maurice Stevenson, Dorance Wedell, Jack Hancock, and Gladys Tallman; (second row) David Aaronson, J. South, unidentified, Edith Kirby, Helen Bowe, Betty Durr, and Jean Aaronson; (third row) Bobby Shinn, Gladys Montrey, unidentified, Wes Kennedy, and Earl Aaronson. (Courtesy of Columbus Grange No. 58.)

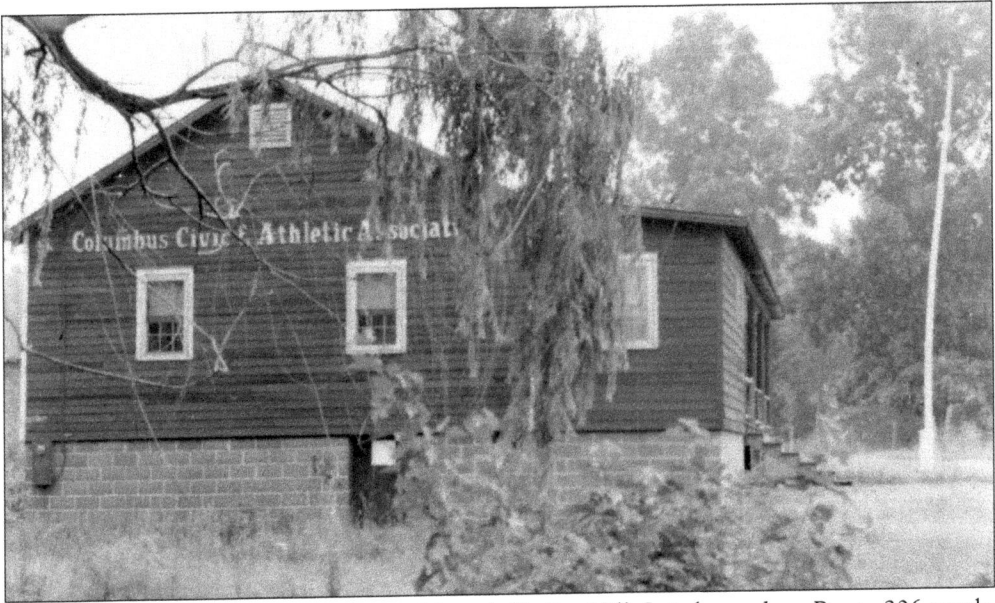

In 1774, this property was the John and Joseph Kerlin Mill. It is located on Route 206 north, outside the town of Columbus. In the early 1900s, George Atkinson operated a sawmill and ice business here. The Columbus Civic and Athletic Association purchased the 14.7 acres on which this building sits from Martin Tusim in 1941. Organized in 1939, the Columbus Civic and Athletic Association sponsored numerous social events on this property. (Courtesy of Mansfield Township Historical Society.)

At a 1950s Christmas party held at the Columbus Civic and Athletic Association, employees and their spouses of the Dzaman Machine Shop, which was located in the old brick Hedding School, enjoy the festivities. Gabriel Dzaman, seated at the head of the table, ran a machine shop that produced cigarette lighters, for which he held patents, and other inventions. (Courtesy of Corinne Hay.)

In this 1940 photograph of a dance class that was held at the IOOF hall on Old York Road west of Hedding, local girls pose. From left to right are Sandra Potts, Jean Bryan, Lois Jaichner, unidentified, Doris Wainwright, Jeanette Roberts, Barbara Cliver, and Alice Jaichner. (Courtesy of Lois Reeves.)

Four young ladies of the Hedding Sew and Save 4-H Club model their fashions for the 1945 Farm Fair at the Walker Gordon Farm. Pictured from left to right are Shirley Bender, Doris Wainwright, Betty Pigott, and Joanne Keiser. (Courtesy of Betty Pigott Wainwright.)

110

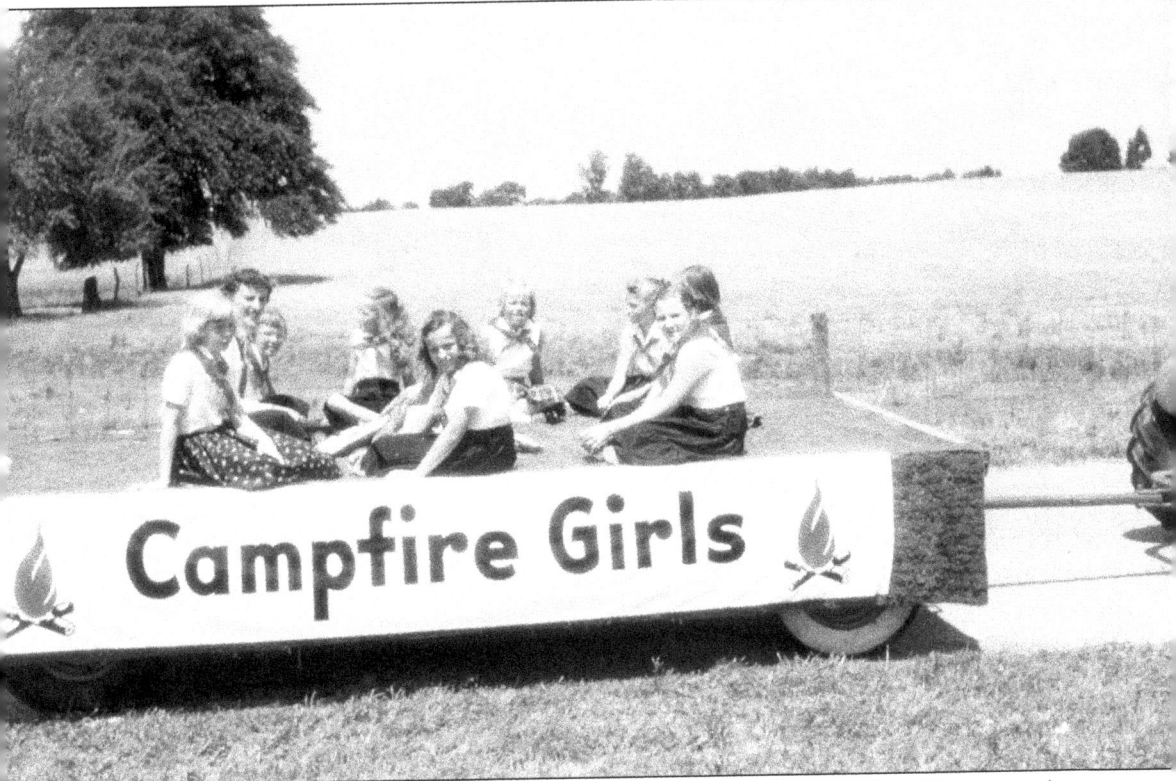

Shown on this Field Day float are young ladies of the Campfire Girls of Columbus. (Courtesy of Ethel Townsend.)

Pictured are the members of the Columbus baseball team. From left to right are (first row) two unidentified men, Ed Carslake, Stanley Townsend, and Gorby Smith; (second row) Ed Rockhill, Bill Archer, and unidentified; (third row) Ben Ridgeway, Harry Titus, Amos Ingling, three unidentified men, and Bill Carslake. At one time, Gorby Smith, who grew up on Locust Avenue in Columbus, played Major League Baseball for the Philadelphia Athletics and the Chicago White Sox. (Courtesy of Janet Aaronson.)

A few members of the Kinkora baseball team gather together with some friends in the background. Henry Jaichner is seated at the far right. (Courtesy of Lois Reeves.)

Members of the 1932 Columbus baseball team included Bud Gilbert, Reds Pew, Carl Matthews, Amos Ingling, Bill Smith, Ed Rockhill, Bill Elliott, Whitey Pew, Ed Smith, Ray Rossell, Spike Danley, and Les Walwyn. (Courtesy of Alice Elliott.)

The 1946 Columbus Athletic Club baseball players, from left to right, are (first row) Wally Reed, Bill Smith, Bill Elliott (manager), batboy Dave Reed (in front), Buck Shonts, Barney Reeves, and Josh Klein; (second row) Les Reed, H. Everham, Bill Pigott, Dick Wedell, Bud Gilbert, Whitey Harrison, George Atkinson, Bill Carslake, and Junior Durr. (Courtesy of Alice Elliott.)

Shown is a group of men from Columbus with a string of rabbits caught during a day of hunting. This was an average amount of rabbits to catch in a day. In the picture, from left to right, are William Carslake, Edward Carslake, their mother Mary Carslake, and Edward's son Edward (Ned) Carslake. The rest of the men are unidentified. (Courtesy of Janet Aaronson.)

Members of the Wytchwood Gunning Club pose with their annual deer hunt. Members in the first row included Frank Potts, Paul Kaufman, Buddy Shreve, and Frank Dewees. In the second row from left to right are George Stanton, Bob Craft, Joe Page, Bill Zelly, Ted Kirby, Clarence Kaufman, Everett Colkitt, and Bill Craft. (Courtesy of Mansfield Township Historical Society.)

The raccoon harvest is on display at the Wytchwood Gunning Club in this photograph from about 1935. The hunters used dogs to track the raccoons. (Courtesy of Rosemary Craft.)

This is the original Short Horn Buck Club cabin in the Jersey Pine Barrens. Other hunt clubs from the area included the Pioneer Gunning Club and Woodmansie. (Courtesy of Hank Reeves.)

The annual deer hunt in December finds the members of the Short Horn Buck Club with a very successful hunt. The Jersey Pine Barrens were well stocked with deer when this picture was taken. The men posing with their catch, from left to right, are Ken Coulter, Bill Aaronson, Gus Montrey, Bud Aaronson, Frank Nutt, Gerald Coulter, Jack Sculley, Bob Carslake, Ted Kirby, and Bill Carslake. (Courtesy of Bob Carslake.)

Four

EVENTS AND
CELEBRATIONS

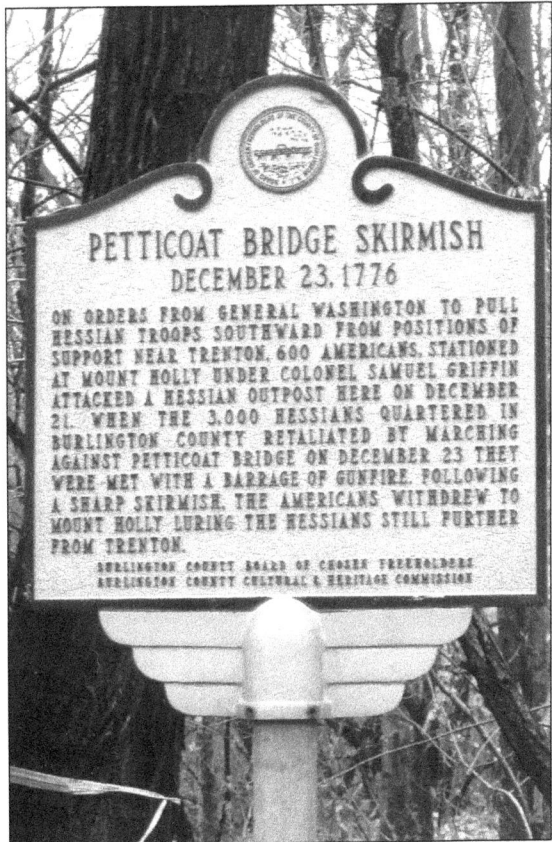

This historic marker is located on the Assiscunk Creek on Petticoat Bridge Road at the bridge crossing. (Courtesy of Marion Tallon.)

With the Columbus and Kinkora Railroad Line depot just a few hundred feet from the Delaware River, the flood of 1903 raised the water level on the rail line six to eight feet above the tracks. It was necessary to transport passengers to and from the trains via a rowboat. (Courtesy of Richard Szatkowski.)

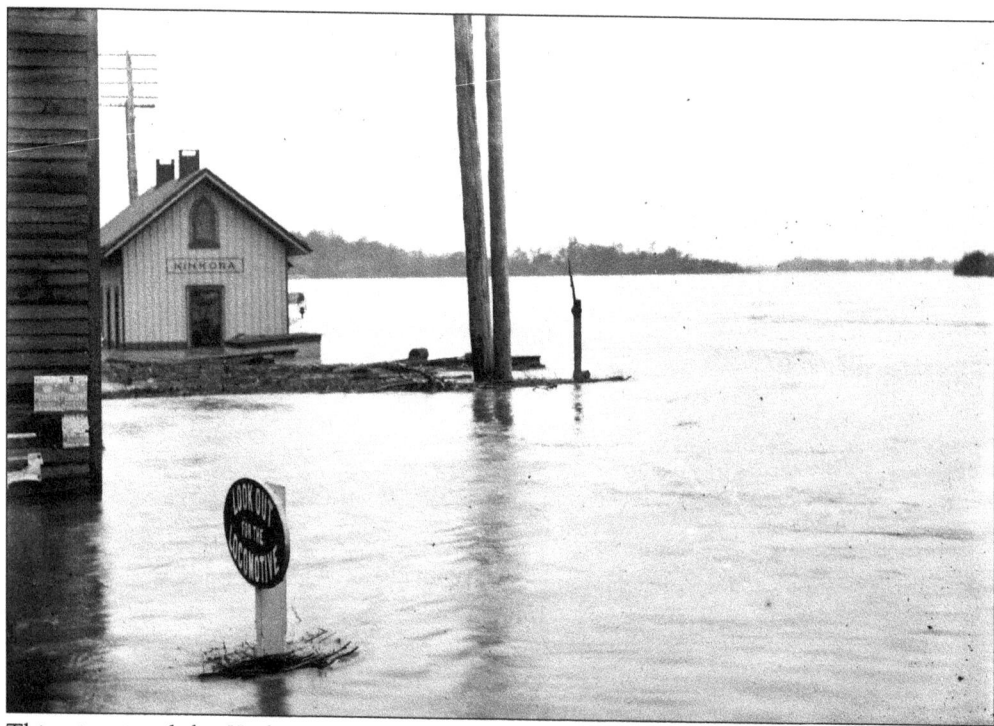

This view is of the Kinkora Railroad station along the Delaware River in the 1903 flood. (Courtesy of Richard Szatkowski.)

Firemen are still hosing down the remains of the C. W. Brick Milling Company on Railroad Avenue in this photograph. The arson fire also destroyed the Columbus Water Company, the Grange League Federation mill, and freight cars loaded with grain on election night, November 9, 1938. Many houses were threatened, but firemen from a dozen surrounding towns fought the devastating blaze. (Courtesy of Franklin Fire Company.)

In this picture from the night of December 28, 1938, firemen struggled to fight the flames at the Grange hall. (Courtesy of Franklin Fire Company.)

Jack Reeves is shown on top of the ladder, Benny Ridgeway is below him, and Bob Townsend is poking in the window to inspect devastation of the original Columbus Grange Hall fire, which was started on December 28, 1938, at 2:45 in the morning and was deemed an arson. (Courtesy of Franklin Fire Company.)

This aerial view of Columbus looking north shows how Route 39 (now Route 206) went through the town. Roger Kirby piloted the plane while John Townsend shot the photograph. (Courtesy of Alfred Kirby.)

Construction work continues on the Route 206 bypass of Columbus. Many houses were razed and a few relocated to make way for the highway. (Courtesy of Mansfield Township Historical Society.)

This aerial view is of Route 206 and the intersection of Old York Road at Rising Sun Square before the New Jersey Turnpike bisected the township. A few farms at the right of the photograph were razed, and Old York Road was rerouted on the west side of Route 206 in the 1950s. (Courtesy of Alfred Kirby.)

Excavation along Mansfield Township is underway for the construction of the New Jersey Turnpike in this picture. (Courtesy of Mansfield Township Historical Society.)

Betty Reeves is shown winning one of the many races at the first Field Day in 1938. Dick Pritchett came in second with Margaret Shonts in third. (Courtesy of Doris DuBell.)

In this line-up of nine men dressed as women for the best-dressed contest for the Field Day in 1938, from left to right, are George Stanton, Roland Armstrong, unidentified, John Haskett, Dick Pritchett, Norman Carty, unidentified, Tom Harvey, and Walter Shonts. (Courtesy of Doris DuBell.)

Nellie Lippincott is shown driving her first place best-decorated tractor in the 1953 Field Day parade. (Courtesy of Ethel Townsend.)

In the best comic division of the parade, one could usually find Borden Shinn and his mother Ethel. Other comic entries who walked for many years were Helen Carslake and Harry George. (Courtesy of Ethel Townsend.)

This picture shows bicycles competing for first prize in the Field Day parade for the decorated bicycle category. They are coming up Atlantic Avenue past the Lippincott farm back into town. (Courtesy of Ethel Townsend.)

Shown is a stagecoach passing the Columbus Inn when it looked like a log cabin with pillars and a wooden balcony. (Courtesy of Mansfield Township Historical Society.)

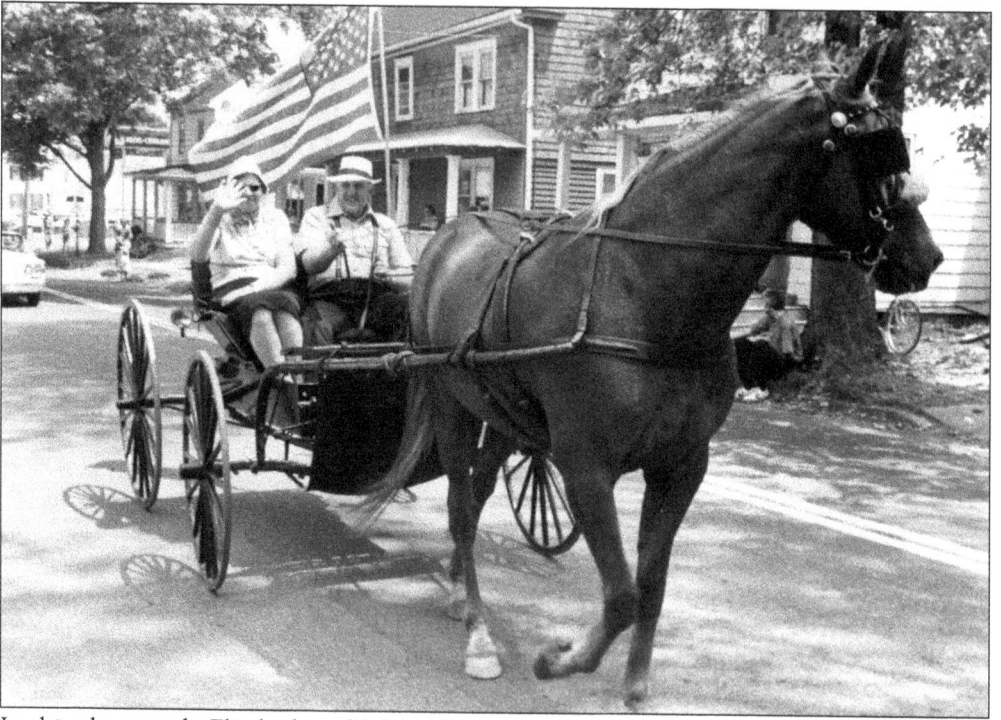

In this photograph, Elizabeth and John Alloway are shown leading the Field Day parade with their horse Steady Franklin. The Alloways led the parade with Steady Franklin pulling the carriage for 25 years. (Courtesy of Elizabeth Alloway.)

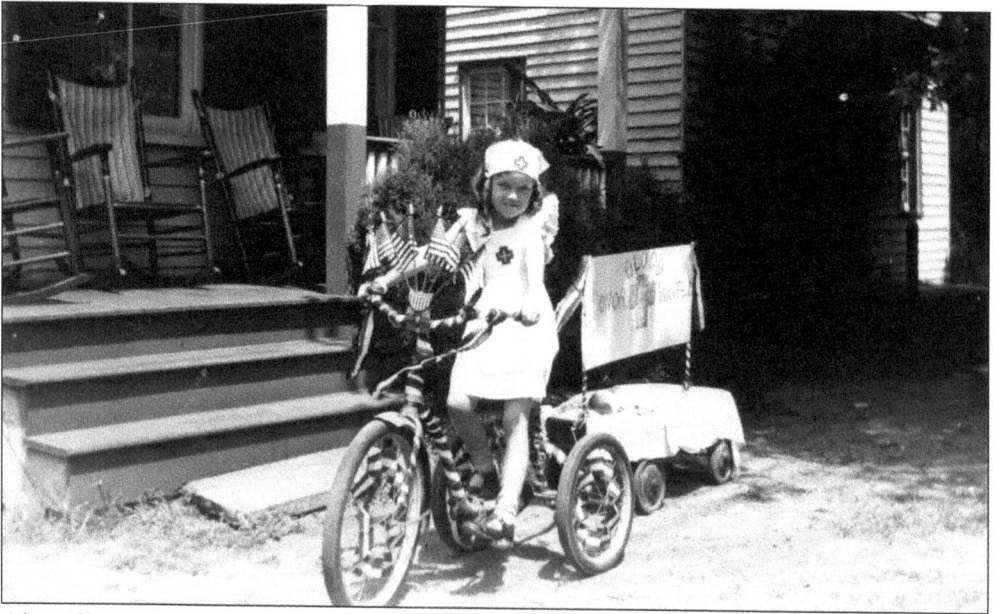

Alice Elliott is shown dressed as an army nurse tending the wounded during World War II in the 1944 Field Day parade. (Courtesy of Alice Elliott.)

Pioneer Gun Club entered its float featuring John Reeves and his wife, Ann, dressed as Davy Crockett and wife in one of the many Field Day parades. Other gun clubs involved each year were Wytchwood, Woodmansie, and Short Horn. (Courtesy of Ethel Townsend.)

Field Day always drew a large crowd from surrounding towns. This scene is near the judge's stand at the corner. Each parade ended with horses. The best draft horses, driving horses, mules, and the best-decorated saddle horse were a part of the parade. Every house with a rose garden had a shovel ready to gather up the free fertilizer. (Courtesy of Ethel Townsend.)

Visit us at
arcadiapublishing.com